Mediterranean Style

Maggie Philo

INTRODUCING STENCILLING

Once you begin stencilling, you will be amazed at the wonderful results you can obtain quite easily and without spending a great deal of money. This book introduces six themed projects and provides ready-to-use stencils that can be used with numerous variations in design – just follow the step-by-step features and simple instructions. With very little paint and only a few pieces of equipment you can achieve stunning results. Have fun!

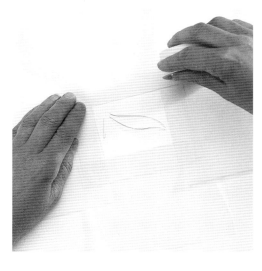

BASIC MATERIALS

Paints and Decorative Finishes
Emulsion paint
Water-based stencil paint
Oil sticks
Acrylic paints (bottles and tubes)
Specialist paints (for fabrics, ceramics, glass etc)
Spray paints
Metallic acrylic artists' colours (gold, silver etc)
Silver and gold art flow pens
Bronze powders (various metallics)
Gilt wax

Brushes and Applicators
Art brushes (variety of sizes)
Stencil brushes (small, medium and large)
Sponge applicators
Mini-roller and tray

Other Equipment
Set square
Blotting paper
Scissors or scalpel (or craft knife)
Roll of lining paper (for practising)
Eraser
Soft pencil
Fine-tip permanent pen
Chalk or Chalkline and powdered chalk
Long rigid ruler
Tape measure
Plumbline
Spirit level
Low-tack masking tape
Spray adhesive
Tracing paper
Paint dishes or palettes
Cloths
Kitchen roll
White spirit
Stencil plastic or card
Cotton buds
Methylated spirit

CUTTING OUT STENCILS
The stencils at the back of the book are all designed to use separately or together to create many different pattern combinations. Cut along the dotted lines of the individual stencils and make sure you transfer the reference code onto each one with a permanent pen. Carefully remove the cut-out pieces of the stencil. Apply 50 mm (2 in) strips of tracing paper around the edges using masking tape; this will help to prevent smudging paint onto your surface.

REPAIRING STENCILS
Stencils may become damaged and torn from mishandling or if the cut-outs have not been removed carefully, but they are easy to repair. Keeping the stencil perfectly flat, cover both sides of the tear with masking tape. Then carefully remove any excess tape with a scalpel.

GETTING STARTED

DUPLICATING STENCILS

Stencil plastic (mylar) can be used or card wiped over with linseed oil, which left to dry will harden and make the surface waterproof. Place the cut-out stencil on top. Trace around carefully with a permanent pen inside the cut-out shapes. Cut along the lines with a scalpel and remove the pieces. You may prefer to trace on top of the design, then transfer your tracing onto card.

MAKING A SPONGE APPLICATOR

Sponging your stencil is one of the easiest methods, but you may prefer to use a stencil brush, especially for fine detail. Using a piece of upholstery foam or dense bath sponge, cut pieces 12–50 mm ($\frac{1}{2}$–2 in) wide and 50 mm (2 in) long. Hold the four corners together and secure with tape to form a pad. You can round off the ends with scissors or a scalpel and trim to a smooth finish. The small-ended applicators can be used for tiny, intricate patterns.

HOW TO USE WATER-BASED PAINT

Water-based paints are easy and economical to use and have the advantage of drying quickly. For professional-looking stencils, do not load your sponge or brush too heavily or you will not achieve a soft, shaded finish. Paint that is too watery will seep under the stencil edges and smudge. If the paint is too heavy, you will obtain a heavy block effect rather than the soft stippling you require.

LOOKING AFTER STENCILS

Stencils have a long life if cared for correctly. Before cleaning, make sure you remove any tape or tracing paper that has been added. Remove any excess paint before it dries and wipe the stencil with a damp cloth every time you use it. If water or acrylic paint has dried and hardened, soften it with water and ease it off gently with a scalpel. Then use a small amount of methylated spirit on a cloth to remove the rest. An oil-based paint can simply be removed by wiping the stencil with white spirit on a cloth. Stencils should be dried thoroughly before storing flat between sheets of greaseproof paper.

HOW TO USE OIL STICKS

Oil sticks may seem expensive but in fact go a long way. They take longer to dry, allowing you to blend colours very effectively. Oil sticks are applied with a stencil brush and you need to have a different brush for each colour. Break the seal as instructed on the stick and rub a patch of the colour onto a palette, allowing space to blend colours. As the stencil sticks dry slowly, you need to lift the stencil off cleanly and replace to continue the pattern.

PRACTISING PAINTING STENCILS

Roll out some lining paper onto a table and select the stencil you wish to practise with. Using spray adhesive, lightly spray the back of your stencil and place it into position on the paper. Prepare your paint on a palette. Dab your sponge or brush into the paint and offload excess paint onto scrap paper. Apply colour over the stencil in a light coat to create an even stippled effect. You can always stencil on a little more paint if a stronger effect is needed, but if you over-apply it in the first place it is very difficult to remove. Keep separate sponges for different colours.

PLANNING YOUR DESIGN

Before starting to stencil, take time to plan your design. Decide where you want to use the patterns, then work out how to position the stencils so that the design will fit around obstacles such as doorways and corners. The techniques shown here will help you to undertake the job with a systematic approach.

MITRING STENCIL PATTERNS

1 Before you apply your design, stencil a sample onto lining paper. Mark the centre and baseline of the design on the paper and put together your pattern pieces. You can then work out the size of the design, how it will fit into the space available and the distance required between repeats.

2 You can avoid stencilling around a corner by working out the number of pattern repeats needed and allowing extra space either between repeats or within the pattern. Creating vertical lines through the pattern will allow you to stretch it evenly.

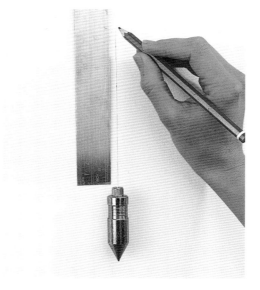

MARKING BASELINES AND HORIZONTAL LINES

Select your stencil area and take a measure from the ceiling, doorframe, window or edging, bearing in mind the depth of your stencil. Using a spirit level, mark out a horizontal line. You can then extend this by using a chalkline or long ruler with chalk or soft pencil.

MARKING VERTICAL LINES

If you need to work out the vertical position for a stencil, hang a plumbline above the stencilling area and use a ruler to draw a vertical line with chalk or a soft pencil. You will need to use this method when creating an all-over wallpaper design.

FIXING THE STENCIL INTO PLACE

Lightly spray the back of the stencil with spray adhesive, then put it in position and smooth it down carefully. You can use low-tack masking tape if you prefer, but take care not to damage the surface to be stencilled; keep the whole stencil flat to prevent paint seeping underneath.

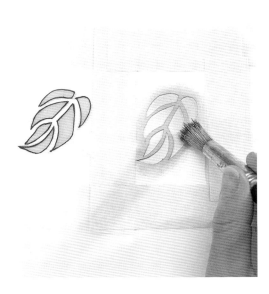  

MARKING THE STENCIL FOR A PATTERN REPEAT

Attach a border of tracing paper to each edge of the stencil. Position the next pattern and overlap the tracing paper onto the previous design, tracing over the edge of it. By matching the tracing with the previous pattern as you work along you will be able to align and repeat the stencil at the same intervals.

COPING WITH CORNERS

Stencil around corners after you have finished the rest of the design, having measured the correct space to leave for the corner pattern before you do so. Then bend the stencil into the corner and mask off one side of it. Stencil the open side and allow the paint to dry, then mask off this half and stencil the other part to complete the design.

MASKING OFF PART OF A STENCIL

Use low-tack masking tape to mask out small or intricate areas of stencil. You can also use ordinary masking tape, but remove excess stickiness first by peeling it on and off your skin or a cloth once or twice. To block off inside shapes and large areas, cut out pieces of tracing paper to the appropriate size and fix them on top with spray adhesive.

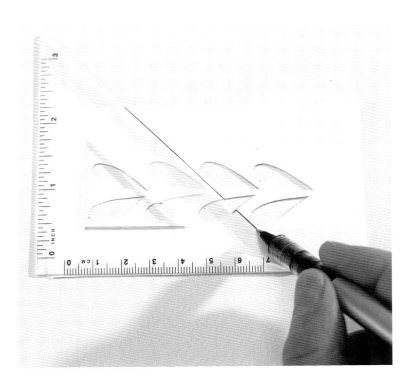 

MITRING STENCIL PATTERNS

1 When you are stencilling a continuous pattern and need to make a corner, mask off the stencil by marking a 45-degree angle on the stencil with a permanent pen. Mask along this line with a piece of masking tape or tracing paper. Stencil up to the mitred corner. Clean the stencil and turn it over so that you can use the reverse side or alternatively cut out another stencil.

2 Make sure the baselines of the stencil on both sides of the corner are the same distance from the edge and that they cross at the corner. Put the diagonal end of the stencil right into the corner and apply the paint. Continue to the next corner and do this in reverse. You may need to create a central motif so that the corners match.

PAINT EFFECTS

CHOOSING COLOURS

Take care to choose appropriate colours to create the effect you want. Stencil a practice piece onto paper and try a variation of colours to ensure you are pleased with the result. Different colours can completely alter a design. Use spray adhesive to fix your practice paper onto the surface on which you wish to produce the design so that you can assess its effect before applying the stencil.

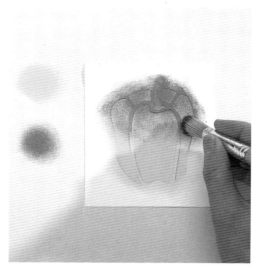

APPLYING WATER-BASED COLOURS

Water-based paint dries quickly, so it tends to layer rather than blend. It is best applied by using a swirling movement or gently dabbing, depending on the finished effect you wish to create. Once you have applied a light base colour, you can add a darker edge for shading. Alternatively, leave some of the stencil bare and add a different tone to that area to obtain a shaded or highlighted appearance.

BLENDING OIL-STICK COLOURS

Oil sticks mix together smoothly and are perfect for blending colours. Place the colours separately on your palette and mix them with white to obtain a variety of tones or blend them together to create new colours. You can also blend by applying one coat into another with a stippling motion while stencilling. Blending looks most effective when applying a pale base coat, then shading on top with a darker colour.

HIGHLIGHTING

A simple way to add highlighting to your design is first to paint in your stencil in a light tone of your main colour, then carefully lift the stencil and move it down a fraction. Then stencil in a darker shade; this leaves the highlighted areas around the top edges of the pattern.

GILDING

After painting your stencil, use gold to highlight the edges. Load a fine art brush with gold acrylic paint and carefully outline the top edges of the pattern. Use one quick brush stroke for each pattern repeat, keeping the same direction. Other methods are to blow bronze powder onto the wet paint, draw around the pattern with a gold flow pen, or smudge on gilt wax cream, then buff to a high sheen.

APPLYING SPRAY PAINTS

Spray paints are ideal on glass, wood, metal, plastic and ceramic surfaces. They are quick to apply and fast drying, but cannot be blended, although you can achieve subtle shaded effects. Apply the paint in several thin coats. Mask off a large area around the design to protect it from the spray, which tends to drift. Try to use sprays out of doors or in a well-ventilated area. Some spray paints are non-toxic, making them ideal for children's furniture.

DIFFERENT SURFACES

BARE WOOD

Rub the wood surface down to a smooth finish. Then fix the stencil in place and paint with a thin base coat of white so that the stencil colours will stand out well when applied. Leave the stencil in place and allow to dry thoroughly, then apply your stencil colours in the normal way. When completely dry, you can apply a coat of light wax or varnish to protect your stencil.

STAINED WOOD

If you are staining wood or medium-density fibreboard (MDF) prior to stencilling, you have a choice of many different wood shades as well as a wide range of colours. If the base coat is dark, stencil a thin coat of white paint on top. Apply your stencil and protect with a coat of clear varnish when it is completely dry.

FABRIC

Use special fabric paint for stencilling on fabric and follow the manufacturer's instructions carefully. Place card or blotting paper behind the fabric while working and keep the material taut. If you are painting a dark fabric, best results are achieved by stencilling first with white or a lighter shade. Heat seal the design following the manufacturer's instructions.

CERAMICS

Use special ceramic paints to work directly onto glazed ceramic tiles and unglazed ceramics such as terracotta. Make sure all surfaces are clean so that the stencils can be fixed easily. Apply the paint with a brush, sponge, spray or mini-roller. Ceramic paints are durable and washable, and full manufacturer's instructions are given on the container.

GLASS

Before applying the stencil make sure the glass is clean, spray on a light coat of adhesive and place the stencil in position. Spray on water-based or ceramic paint, remove the stencil and allow to dry. If you wish to stencil drinking glasses, use special non-toxic and water-resistant glass paints. An etched-glass look with stencils on windows, doors and mirrors can be achieved with a variety of materials.

PAINTED SURFACES

Stencils can be applied to surfaces painted with matt, satin or vinyl silk emulsion, oil scumble glazes, acrylic glazes and varnishes, and to matt wallpaper. If you wish to decorate a gloss surface, stencil first with an acrylic primer, leave to dry and then stencil the colours on top. Surfaces to be stencilled need to be smooth so that the stencil can lay flat.

SUNFLOWER TABLECLOTH

Stencilling with fabric paints is a lovely and creative way to add colour to plain white table linen and make it unique. The sunflower border around the hem is composed of quite a large number of individual stencils and you may find it much easier to trace all the components and make your own stencil. This is a particularly good idea if you are working on cloth, as you cannot usually remove the fabric paint once it has been applied. This sunflower tablecloth will enliven your table and add a summer feeling to your meals.

PAINT COLOUR GUIDE

Bright yellow   Leaf green   Dark brown

STENCILLING ON FABRIC

1 Measure the cloth and work out how many sunflowers will fit length- and widthways, allowing enough space for the corner motif. Adjust the distance between stems if necessary.

2 Stencil the sunflowers, bees and leaves with the appropriate fabric colour. The dark brown flower centres and stripes on the bees can be stencilled over the yellow paint to avoid masking out these areas.

3 Iron the tablecloth on the reverse side to fix the fabric paint, according to the manufacturer's instructions.

PROJECT PATTERN
The design around the bottom of the tablecloth is a repeat of this arrangement.

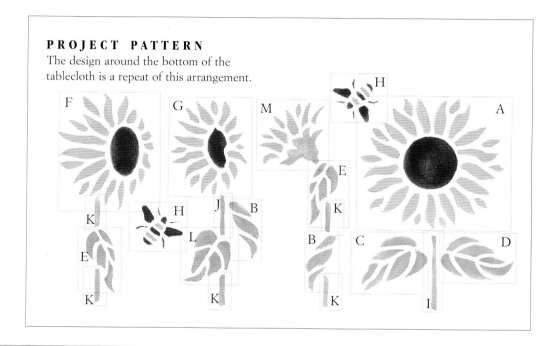

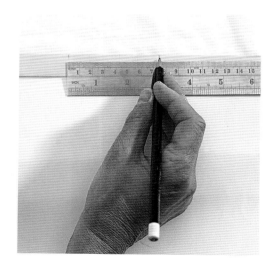

MARKING OUT THE PATTERN
Strips of masking tape are stuck along each hem edge of the cloth. This forms a base line over which the sunflower stems will be positioned. Use a pencil and ruler to mark the pattern repeat along the masking tape.

PAINTING THE FLOWER CENTRES
Place a tracing paper mask over the stencil card when stencilling the centres to prevent the paint from colouring the petals. To make a mask, trace around the centre of each sunflower on the stencil cards, then cut each of them just outside the traced lines.

STENCILLING THE CORNERS
The large sunflower head is used as a cornerpiece for the border design. Check accurate positioning with a ruler or set square before completing each corner of the cloth with the design.

SUNFLOWER TABLECLOTH VARIATIONS

Simply by changing the stencil colours – using purple or another colour instead of yellow, or stencilling a green centre – the sunflowers can appear to be a variety of chrysanthemums or daisies. The large sunflower head would be an excellent choice for an all-over wall pattern. The bee motif is very popular and can be used to embellish a variety of decorative accessories. It would also look stunning on stationery.

SMALL SUNFLOWER HEADS (STENCIL A)

SPIRALLING LEAVES (STENCIL B)

SUNFLOWER HEADS WITH GREY CENTRES (STENCIL A)

BLUE SUNFLOWERS (STENCIL G)

BEE AND LEAF BORDER (STENCILS H AND L)

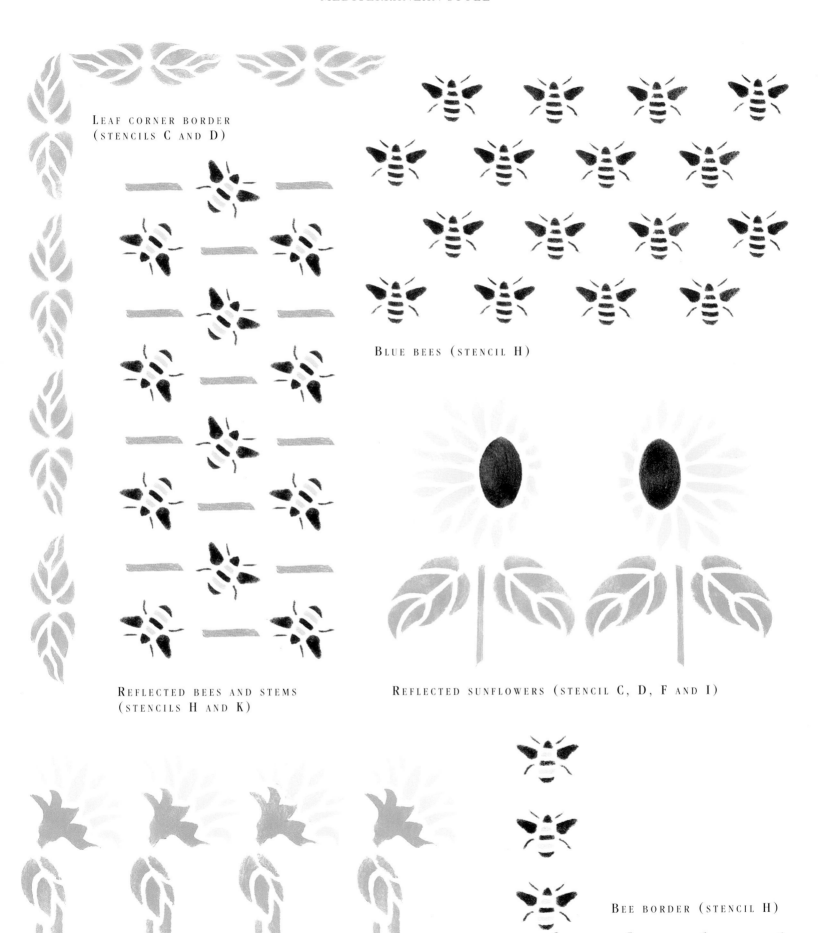

LEAF CORNER BORDER
(STENCILS C AND D)

BLUE BEES (STENCIL H)

REFLECTED BEES AND STEMS
(STENCILS H AND K)

REFLECTED SUNFLOWERS (STENCIL C, D, F AND I)

BEE BORDER (STENCIL H)

HALF-OPEN SUNFLOWERS (STENCILS E, K AND M)

OLIVE BORDER

The classic border of black olives was inspired by a frieze found in a Tuscan country house. The combination of the wall and stencil colours used in this particular pattern provides an extremely soft look. However, if you prefer, you could make the effect even more subtle by taking the golden olive colour applied to the top and bottom of the design and using this to stencil the olives. The design can also successfully be flipped in order to make vertical stripes, perhaps to complete either co-ordinating curtains or a blind.

PAINT COLOUR GUIDE

Ultramarine blue*   Paynes grey
Alizarin crimson*   Golden olive green
Burnt umber*   Olive green
Oxide of chromium green   *mix to make aubergine

PAINTING THE BORDER

1 Paint the wall white and when dry, paint over with one coat of cream-coloured emulsion paint to create a slightly patchy effect.

2 Mark horizontal pencil lines where you will place stencil D, both above and below the olive design. Use a spirit level to check accuracy.

3 Stencil the top and bottom of the border (stencils D and E) with golden olive colour and apply the other shades to the olive design.

PROJECT PATTERN
The dado border in the photograph opposite is a repeat pattern of this arrangement.

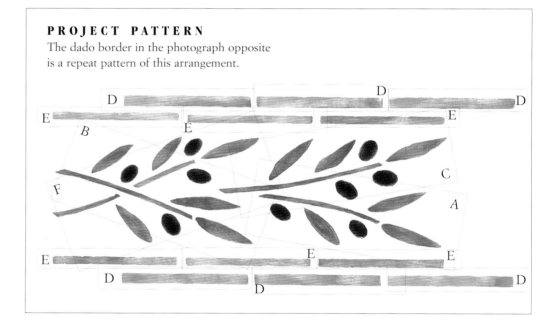

POSITIONING THE BORDER REPEAT
To enable you to position and repeat the border design accurately, trace the stencil cards and attach the traced design to the card with masking tape.

PAINTING THE LEAVES
Stick a strip of masking tape over each of the olives before stencilling the leaves to protect them from the green paint. The olive-green shade can then be safely applied.

APPLYING SHADING
Shading is applied to the leaves and olives to give a soft three-dimensional appearance. Oxide of chromium green is applied sparingly over the olive base on the leaves, and paynes grey paint is stencilled over the aubergine-coloured olives.

OLIVE BORDER VARIATIONS

Olives lend themselves well to subtle colour schemes, using natural earth colours. By adding leaves and extra olives you can extend the size of the branches and they can be made endlessly adaptable. Although they are used in a bedroom environment in the main project, the stencils are particularly appropriate for decorating either a kitchen or dining room and would also look very attractive on table mats.

DECORATIVE BORDER (STENCILS D, E AND PART OF F)

GOLDEN OLIVE FRIEZE (PARTS OF STENCIL C)

DARK OLIVE FRIEZE (STENCIL F)

OLIVE AND LEAF REPEAT
(STENCIL C)

OLIVE BRANCH BORDER
(STENCIL F)

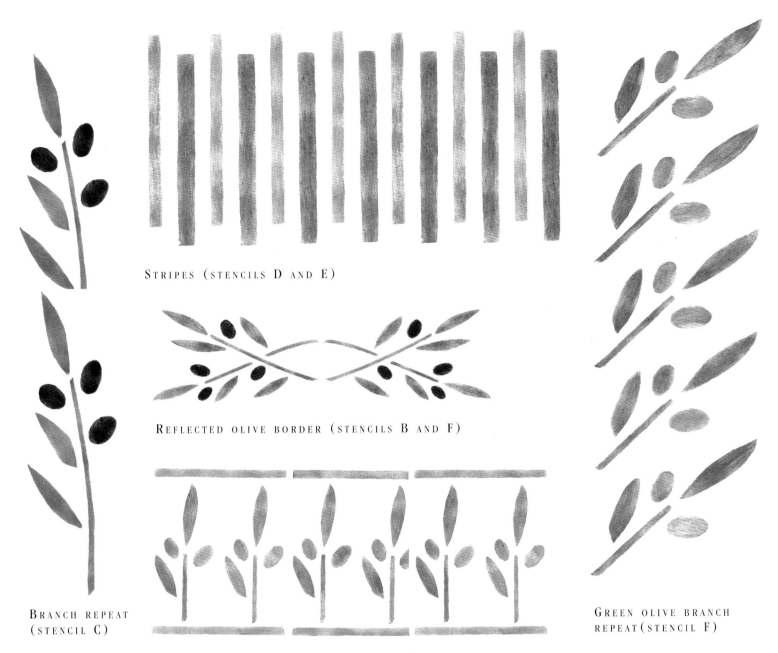

Stripes (stencils D and E)

Reflected olive border (stencils B and F)

Branch repeat (stencil C)

Standing pattern (stencils E and F)

Green olive branch repeat (stencil F)

Decorative frieze (stencils D, E and F)

GERANIUM FRIEZE

PAINT COLOUR GUIDE

Deep red	Yellow ochre	Mid green
Dark green	Terracotta	White
Chestnut brown		

PAINTING THE FRIEZE

1 Paint the wall with two coats of white paint. Using a pencil, ruler and spirit level, mark a horizontal line along the bottom of the wall where you want the base of the flower pots to be.

2 Stencil the pots using terracotta then chestnut brown. Place the pots randomly, leaving room between each for the geraniums.

3 Stencil the leaves and stems with the yellow and green paint. Use two or three leaves to complete the width and three or four for the height. Finish with one or two flower heads.

B righten up a boring outside wall with a frieze of colourful geraniums that will remain in bloom throughout the year. The leaf stencil cards are used both sides to balance the designs but they can also be placed more randomly. However, if you prefer an exact arrangement you can trace a complete design, and use the tracing held in place to slot each leaf card in the correct position for stencilling. Given time, the design should acquire an attractive weathered appearance. To extend the life of your stencil, finish the pattern with two or three coats of an exterior varnish. You could also use this stencil inside the house – it would look good on a kitchen or dining room wall.

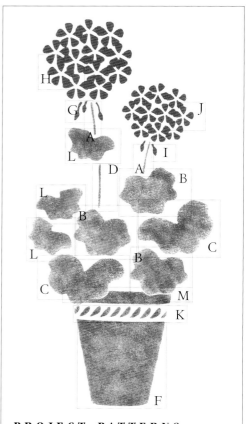

PROJECT PATTERNS
This arrangement forms the design for the pot of geraniums on the left of the picture opposite.

PAINTING OVERHANGING LEAVES
To allow the leaves to appear to hang over the edges of the flowerpots, you will first need to stencil the leaf with white paint. Apply this where the design overlaps the pot to blot out the terracotta colour.

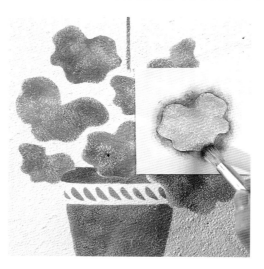

STENCILLING THE LEAVES
Give dimension to the leaves by stencilling first with yellow ochre, and then, more sparingly, with one or two shades of green paint. You can add variety to the frieze by altering the proportions of colour slightly from pot to pot.

PAINTING THE FLOWERS
The petals of the geranium flowers are built up by repeating the petal stencil randomly to form a roughly circular shape. This necessitates overlapping the design here and there as you stencil.

16

GERANIUM FRIEZE VARIATIONS

The petal arrangement on the geranium flower head is extremely versatile and can be laid out in a large number of ways. When the motif is used on its own, it becomes a stylized flower and can be stencilled in any colour to suit your selected scheme. The decorative band used in the flower pot forms a repeat pattern and is ideal for positioning the side of a border or a stripe design. This particular flower pot pattern will enable you to vary the motifs considerably and if you are in a creative mood, both surprising and spectacular results will ensue.

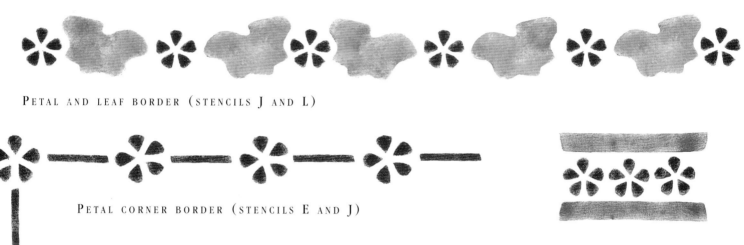

PETAL AND LEAF BORDER (STENCILS J AND L)

PETAL CORNER BORDER (STENCILS E AND J)

GERANIUM WITH LEAF REPEAT
(STENCILS D, H AND L)

PETAL STRIPE
(STENCILS J AND M)

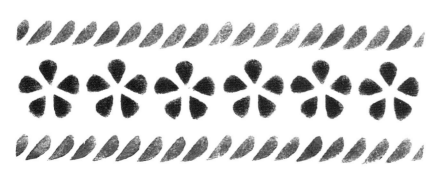

PETAL AND LEAF REPEAT (STENCILS H AND K)

PETAL BOX (STENCILS H AND M)

GERANIUM REPEAT (STENCILS D, G, H AND I)

FLOWER AND LEAF ZIG ZAG (STENCILS B AND J)

FLOWER POT
(STENCILS E, F AND H)

ALTERNATE FLOWER SIZES BORDER (STENCILS H AND J)

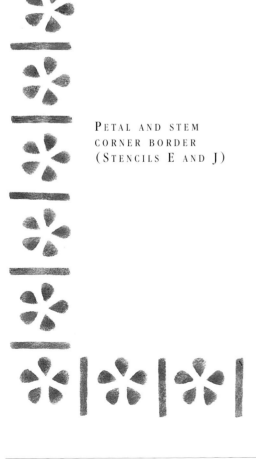

PETAL AND STEM
CORNER BORDER
(STENCILS E AND J)

FLOWER TILES (STENCILS D AND H)

LEAF BORDER (STENCIL C)

TERRACOTTA POTS

U nglazed terracotta does not require special ceramic paint and stencilling pots is a simple way to give an inexpensive item a more stylish appearance. The square flower pots shown opposite are very simple to complete, although the circular dish is a little more tricky, as the stencilling can be seen from all angles and the design has to fit around the surface exactly. Because the surface is gently curved, you will need to use your hand to ease the stencil cards into place as you go. Start with the small square flower pots to get a feel for the pattern before you work on the circular dish.

PAINT COLOUR GUIDE

Ultramarine blue*   Cadmium red
Alizarin crimson*   Cobalt blue
Oxide of chromium green Burnt umber*
*mix to make aubergine

PAINTING THE POTS

1 Trace the cherry tomato design and attach to the stencil card. The tracing should be at the correct distance to create a repeat that fits exactly around the dish. (See step 2 below.)

2 Stencil the tomatoes then apply the blue rim and aubergine designs on the inside of the bowl, using the same technique as in step 1.

3 Complete by painting a blue stripe around the base of the bowl to balance the design.

PROJECT PATTERNS
A repeat of the arrangement on top forms the design on the inside of the bowl. The design around the outside is a repeat of the arrangement below.

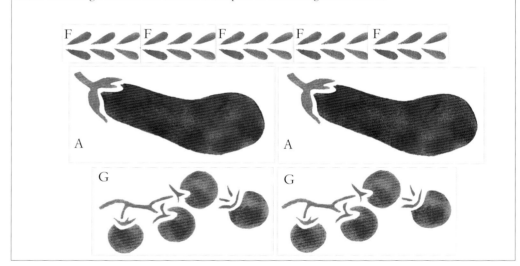

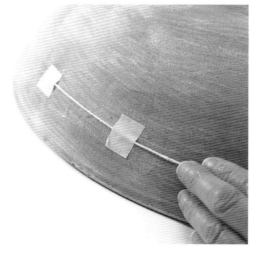

PAINTING THE POT
You can tone down the bright colour of new terracotta by brushing over with diluted white emulsion paint. Brush approximately 1 part paint to 10 parts water around the inside and outside of the bowl.

MEASURING THE REPEAT
To work out the number of repeats of the cherry tomato stencil that are required, tape a piece of string around the circumference of the bowl then measure its length. Divide the width of the tomato stencil into this measurement and adjust the space between each accordingly.

PAINTING THE BORDER
Brush a border around the base of the bowl with a stencil brush. An easy way to make sure the line is even is to place three strips of tape adjacent to each other, then remove the central strip.

TERRACOTTA POTS VARIATIONS

The vegetable stencil cards are very adaptable as each one is a figurative design and can be used independently. The design would be perfect for decorating all kinds of kitchen storage jars and containers. Try them on glassware or white china to add a splash of colour, or use them to brighten up plain garden pots. They would also be perfect patterns to decorate tablecloths and place mats for an outdoor summer table.

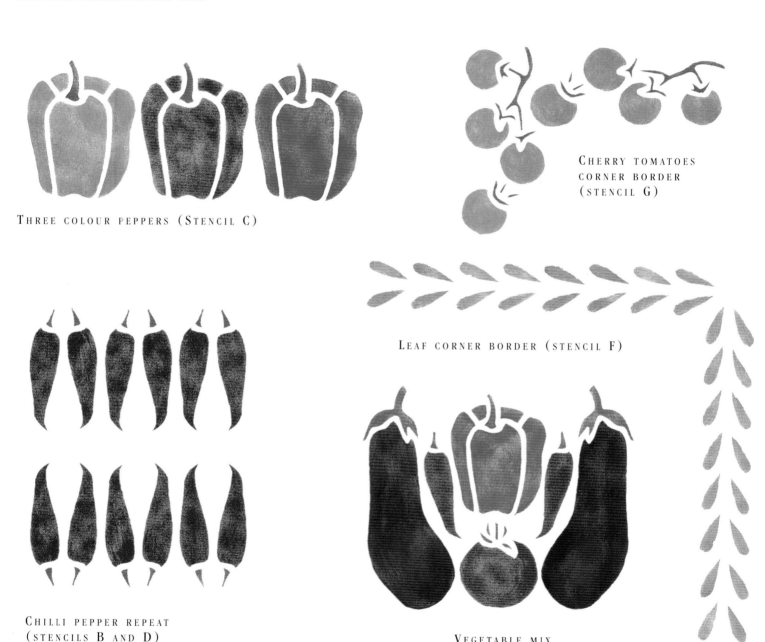

THREE COLOUR PEPPERS (STENCIL C)

CHERRY TOMATOES
CORNER BORDER
(STENCIL G)

LEAF CORNER BORDER (STENCIL F)

CHILLI PEPPER REPEAT
(STENCILS B AND D)

VEGETABLE MIX
(STENCILS A, B, C, D AND E)

CHILLI PEPPER STRIPE (STENCILS B AND D)

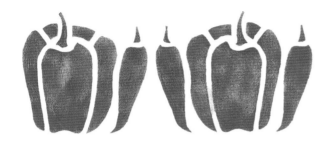

PEPPER AND CHILLI BORDER
(STENCILS B, C AND D)

REFLECTED CHILLI PATTERN (STENCILS B, D AND G)

REFLECTED LEAF STRIPE (STENCIL F)

PEPPER AND TOMATO REPEAT (STENCILS C AND E)

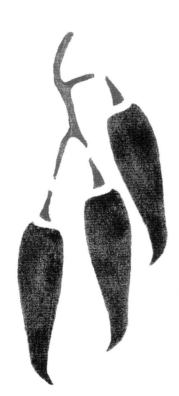

GREEN TOMATOES (STENCIL G)

TOMATO REPEAT (STENCIL E)

CHERRY TOMATO
BORDER
(STENCIL G)

CHILLI PEPPER MOTIF
(STENCILS B, D AND G)

PAINT COLOUR GUIDE

Lemon yellow	Bright orange
Oxide of chromium green	Burnt umber

PAINTING THE WALL

1 Paint the wall with two coats of white silk emulsion paint and apply a deep blue colourwash on top.

2 Mark the wall where the tree will be positioned at the height you require. Drop a plumb line to mark the centre of the tree.

3 Arrange the shapes on the wall starting at the top of the design. Adjust the length of the trunk by repeating the middle section (Stencil D) as required. Start applying paint when you are pleased with the arrangement.

ORANGE TREE

An uneven rustic wall provides a surface that is wonderfully quick and easy to colourwash and gives a very attractive appearance to the stencil work. The whole of the design is first stencilled with lemon yellow paint, which is slightly opaque. This provides a good base, on the strong blue surface, for stencilling the other colours. The layering of paint colours (yellow, orange and green) gives the whole stencil a shaded effect, making the tree look more three-dimensional. You can copy the arrangement as shown exactly, but if you prefer to plan your own design, it is better to start with the oranges, then build the leaf shapes around these.

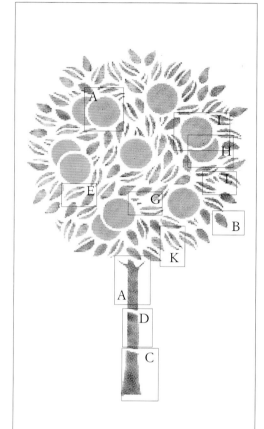

PROJECT PATTERN

The orange tree in the picture opposite has been stencilled using this arrangement.

APPLYING A COLOURWASH
A colourwash can be made by thinning emulsion paint with about six parts water. Use a household sponge to apply the wash to a textured wall, using plenty of arm movement, as though you were cleaning it.

PLANNING THE DESIGN
The easiest way to plan a design that contains many elements is to duplicate each stencil on a piece of paper, draw inside the stencil card and photocopy the designs several times. Roughly cut out the paper shapes and use a re-positional spray adhesive to attach them to the wall.

STENCILLING THE COLOUR
To stencil the design accurately, simply remove one paper shape at a time and position the stencil card in its place. Then apply the yellow base colour followed by the second shade as appropriate.

ORANGE TREE VARIATIONS

The oranges have not been used to represent fruit in these designs, but instead form geometric arrangements for borders and stripes. Unnatural turquoise and lime green shades have been used for some leaf variations, giving them a vibrant and contemporary appearance. Try linking a variety of leaves with a freehand painted stem using a fine artist's brush.

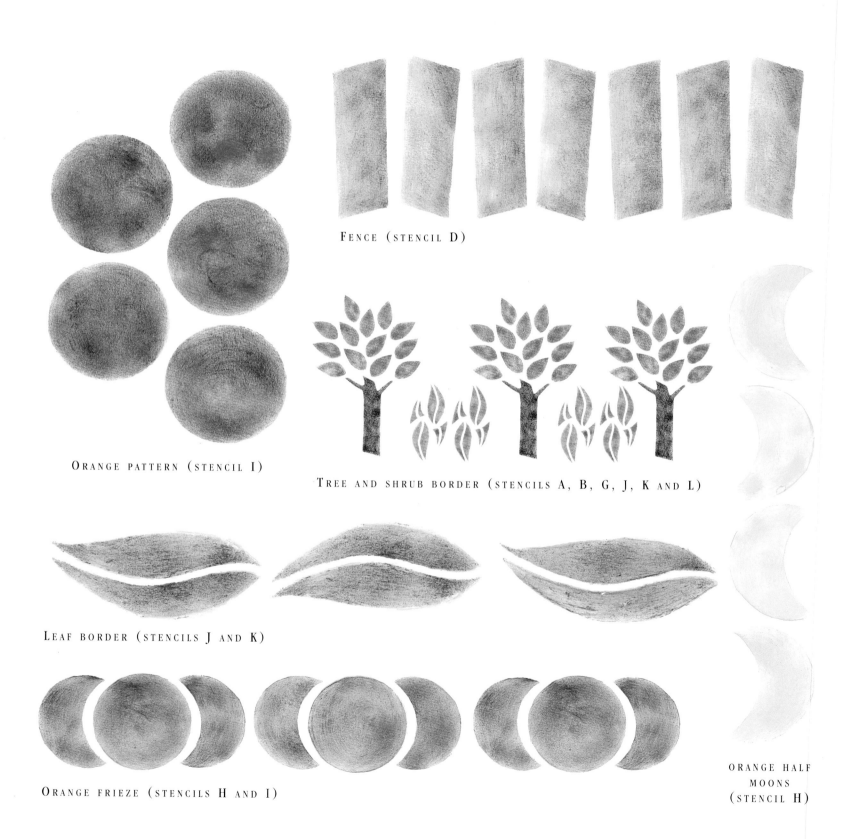

FENCE (STENCIL D)

ORANGE PATTERN (STENCIL I)

TREE AND SHRUB BORDER (STENCILS A, B, G, J, K AND L)

LEAF BORDER (STENCILS J AND K)

ORANGE FRIEZE (STENCILS H AND I)

ORANGE HALF MOONS (STENCIL H)

ORNAMENTAL LEAF REPEAT (STENCILS G, J, K AND L)

REFLECTED LEAF PATTERN (STENCILS E AND F)

TREE MOTIF
(STENCILS A AND B)

ORNAMENTAL LEAF FRIEZE (STENCILS E, F, J AND K)

BUD MOTIF
(STENCILS E AND F)

BUD BORDER (STENCILS B, E AND F)

PORTUGUESE FISHING BOATS

The mock tiles are quick to stencil and look very effective, but for a good result, time needs to be spent on careful marking out, with the help of a spirit level. Stencilling the design onto an existing tiled wall would obviously be quicker and would be an excellent way to update the appearance. Make sure you use appropriate paint and primers if you choose this option. If you want the surface to be more durable, you could stencil the designs onto new tiles using ceramic paint and cure them in an oven.

PAINT COLOUR GUIDE

Prussian blue   Burnt sienna

PAINTING THE TILES

1 Paint the wall with pale blossom pink silk emulsion paint. Place a strip of masking tape horizontally on the wall forming the tiled area.

2 Mark out and mask the tiled area and create the mock tile effect by brushing on scumble glaze coloured with red ochre acrylic paint. Stencil the tiles randomly using the two paint colours to produce a shaded effect.

3 Remove all the masking tape and rub out the pencil marks. To create a contrasting band of colour above the tiles, mask off the area and brush on a blue grey paint glaze.

PROJECT PATTERN
This arrangement, repeated at random, forms the tile pattern in the photograph opposite.

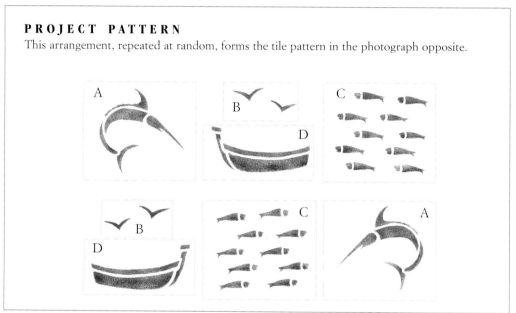

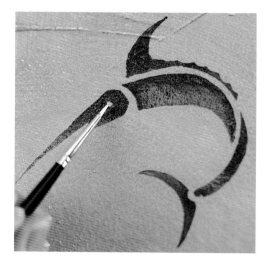

MARKING OUT THE TILES
To create mock grouting, draw horizontal lines on the wall at approximately 13 cm (5 in) intervals, then mark vertical lines in the same way to form a grid. Place fine line or car striping tape over the marked-out squares.

CREATING A TILE EFFECT
A tile effect can be achieved by brushing on a coloured glaze over the masked area of the wall. Mix acrylic paint with acrylic scumble glaze to the required depth of colour. Apply the glaze thinly to the wall, brushing over the brush marks to soften the effect.

PAINTING THE FISH
The eyes on the swordfish and shoals of small fish cannot be cut as part of the stencil. However you can paint them on to provide additional detail, using a fine pointed artist's brush and the blossom pink wall paint.

PORTUGUESE FISHING BOATS VARIATIONS

The fish and boats pictured here have been stencilled with brighter colours than those in the main project. Although a bathroom is the obvious room for sea designs, the boats in particular would look wonderful in a child's room. Try masking off sections of the boat and stencil the different parts with stormy primary colours. The leaping swordfish can be used at any angle you wish to indicate direction of movement.

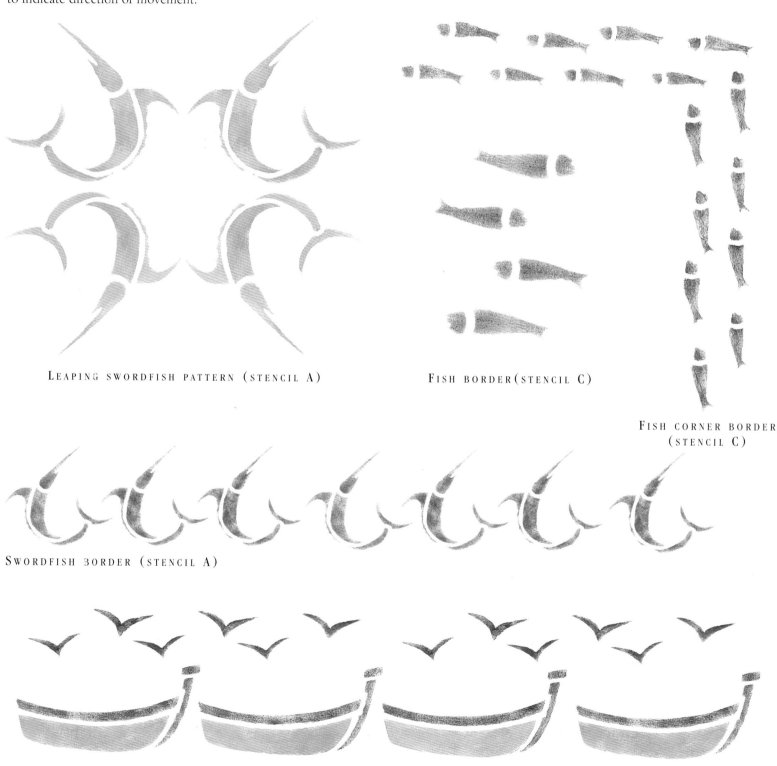

LEAPING SWORDFISH PATTERN (STENCIL A)

FISH BORDER (STENCIL C)

FISH CORNER BORDER
(STENCIL C)

SWORDFISH BORDER (STENCIL A)

BOAT AND SEAGULL BORDER (STENCILS B AND D)

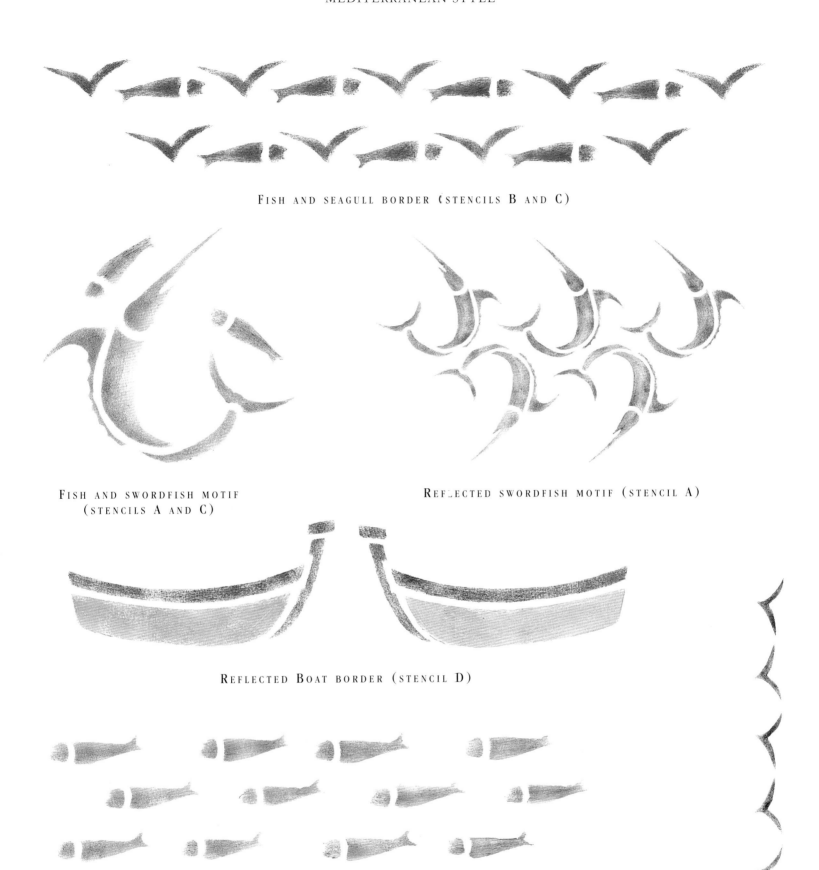

FISH AND SEAGULL BORDER (STENCILS B AND C)

FISH AND SWORDFISH MOTIF
(STENCILS A AND C)

REFLECTED SWORDFISH MOTIF (STENCIL A)

REFLECTED BOAT BORDER (STENCIL D)

SHOAL OF FISH (STENCIL C)

SEAGULL BORDER (STENCIL B)

SUPPLIERS

A. S. Handover
37 Mildmay Grove
London
N1 4RH
Tel: 0207 359 4696

Green and Stone
259 Kings Road
Chelsea
London
SW3 5EL
Tel: 0207 352 0837

Stencil Store Company Ltd
20–21 Heronsgate Road
Chorleywood
Hertfordshire
WD3 5BN
Tel: 01923 285 577/8

London Graphic Centre
16–18 Shelton Street
London
WC2H 9JJ
Tel: 0207 240 0095

ACKNOWLEDGEMENTS

First published in 2001 by Murdoch Books (UK) Ltd

ISBN 1-85391-878 4
A catalogue record of this book is available from the British Library.
Text and photography © Murdoch Books (UK) Ltd

Commissioning Editor: Natasha Martyn-Johns
Senior Project Editor: Anna Osborn
Senior Designer: Helen Taylor
Photography: Graham Ainscough
Stylist: Caroline Davis

CEO: Robert Oerton
Publisher: Catie Ziller
Publishing Manager: Fia Fornari
Production Manager: Lucy Byrne

Group General Manager: Mark Smith
Group CEO/Publisher: Anne Wilson

Colour separation by Colourscan in Singapore
Printed in China through Phoenix Offset

Murdoch Books (UK) Ltd
Ferry House, 51–57 Lacy Road,
Putney, London, SW15 1PR
Tel: +44 (0)20 8355 1480, Fax: +44 (0)20 8355 1499
Murdoch Books (UK) Ltd is a subsidiary
of Murdoch Magazines Pty Ltd.

Murdoch Books®
GPO Box 1203
Sydney, Australia, NSW 1045
Tel: +61 (0)2 4352 7025, Fax: +61 (0)2 4352 7026
Murdoch Books® is a trademark of Murdoch
Magazines Pty Ltd.

Maggie Philo is a designer with many years experience working with a wide variety of decorative paint finishes for
walls and furniture. She is an experienced teacher of paint effects and other techniques including gilding, stencilling
and découpage. In 1993, she began selling her unique range of découpaged designs at major fairs including the
Country Living Fair, the House and Garden Fair, and the Homes and Gardens Grand Sales. Maggie is the author of
10 books, including *Decorative Painted Furniture* and *Traditional Borders*, and regularly contributes to homecraft
magazines. She has also appeared on daytime television programmes demonstrating decorative techniques, made a
video, and given talks and demonstrations at numerous exhibitions and events.